THE GIFT

BY

ANITHA MARIE GREVERIUS

Title: The Gift
Author: © 2022, Anitha Marie Greverius
Editor: Hagens Skrivbyrå, Eskilstuna Sweden
Translator: Amanda Tedenljung
ISBN: 978-91-8007-806-1
Publisher: BoD – Books on Demand, Stockholm, Sweden
Print: BoD - Books On Demand, Norderstedt, Germany

CONTENTS

FORWARD TO THE GIFT

In Anitha's book, the Gift, she shows us what an intimate, personal relationship with God can be like. He is not a God far off, distant and uncaring, but rather He is a Father, concerned about our needs, our challenges and our difficulties. He comes into our lives with exactly the gift that we need at the right time.

James 1:17 "Every good gift and every perfect gift is from above and cometh down from the Father of lights, with whom is no variableness neither shadow of turning."

One of the things that we learn as we walk through life, is that so much of what we have (health, possessions, peace, relationships, etc.) are gifts from God. He is so incredibly generous and He gives us these wonderful things, as a way of showing us that he loves us.

Luke 12: 32 "Fear not, little flock, for it is your Father's good pleasure to give to you His Kingdom." We also see that He delights in giving to us, the things of His kingdom. It actually gives Him great pleasure to take what He has and to give it to us.

No better example of this is to be found, than in the gift of His

Son. *John 3: 16* "For God so loved the world, that He gave His only begotten Son, that whosoever believes in Him, should not perish but have everlasting life."

He does not want us to perish, so he has given to us: His Son, to rescue us. So that we might enjoy eternal life.
And, if that wasn't enough, He has promised to freely give us all things WITH His Son.

Rom 8:32 "He who spared not His own Son, but delivered him up for us all, how will He not also along with him freely give us all things?" So, what is our part, you may ask? To receive. He is coming to us each day with wonderful gifts. May you take them and use them as a blessing in your life and to bless others too.

My hope is that as you read "The Gift," you too will begin to experience what it can mean to walk with the Son each day.

 **Jack Kody,** Washington, USA, founder of Crossroad Foundational Ministries and bible teacher of Youth With a Mission.

PREFACE BY THE AUTHOR

bout me.

This book came to me during a time of reflection and stillness. One evening I felt how a strong flow of words – an even stream– came upon me, as through a vision. When I sat down by my computer, it was as if someone delivered the story for me to write. "The Encounter with the Giver" was at first supposed to be an inspirational book, written to those who are seeking, primarily those who had already experienced something spiritual.

In my prayers, I gave the story to God and asked for help editing it. A short while later I visited my good friend Fia, who immediately offered her assistance to edit it, as she already had experience of writing and editing textbooks. The joy I felt when I realised that there was a purpose with this little book was tremendous. Not long thereafter, there was a request from Fia's daughter Amanda, who is a professional translator, to translate this book into English.

I prayed that a renowned and appreciated author or preacher would write the preface to "The Gift". My prayers were answered, when Jack Kody, USA, was invited to the Salvation Army's Training School "Saved2Save", situated in Visby. The theme of Jack Kody's teachings was "God's fatherly heart", something that Jack Kody loves preaching about. Kody is the founder of Crossroad Foundational Ministries, was previously a missionary and is still active within Youth with a Mission. Kody read my book and became very interested, so when I requested him to write the preface to the book "The Gift", he accepted.

Since the end of the 90's I have been a salvationist myself and was often hired to preach and to teach at the Salvation Army in Visby, in women's groups and prayer gatherings as well as at Christian retreats. I am a single parent with two adult children and five grandchildren. I live in a two-bedroom apartment in Visby with a brilliant view over the sea.

To this day, I work as a specialist nurse in psychiatry, which is a profession that I love dearly. The heavy impact our words have on other people never ceases to amaze me, whether they are of encouragement, affirmation or offence, which degrades. The focus of my teachings is often God's love and ability to heal, something that I have found to be crucial for those that I meet in the psychiatric ward. There, many have scarred souls. Among people today, there is a hunger for meaning and goals in life.

The purpose of this book is to act as inspiration and encouragement for us to receive the gifts of God and the life purpose He has intended for every person.

Anitha Marie Greverius

Author and Inspirer

"Och så öppnades en port" ('And then a door was opened'-
translators' notes). Illustration inspired by a water coloured
painting made by Lillemor Carlsén, 1998

THE GIFT

For with You is the fountain of life; in Your light do we see light.
Psalm 36:9

With eyes filled with unconditional love, He handed me the beaker. The golden liquid residing in it glistened in the light radiating from Him. The beverage had the taste of a blend of honey and roses, however, once I had swallowed I felt as if a dagger of light and dark tore through my soul. Lightness and darkness, delectable divine messages mixed with horrific visions travelled through me alike a hurtful stream. I could see crying people and I could feel the pain in their souls. Even sentiments of greatest pleasure shot straight through me and had me blink away tears of joy, running down my blushing cheeks like hot rivers. The two-edged sword sliced my soul apart.

"*What* was it that you gave me?" I uttered with a gasp. "What was it that you gave me that could make me feel both grief and bliss?"

The creature leaned over and removed the beaker, now empty, from my hands. Its eyes were large and mild, resembling bright, bottomless pools of adoration.

"I gave to you a part of the heavenly vision, my daughter." "Are you an angel...?" I asked. However, in my mind I asked myself the words I would not dare speak aloud: "...or are you a demon?" The creature shimmered in all of the colours of the rainbow each time he moved.

"I am a messenger from the heavenly throne," said He, kindly and honourably. "I have come to give you The Gift; the very same Gift that was pre-determinedly yours even before you were born; the Gift that opens doors; that provides wisdom; that grants vision to the visionless; the Gift that allows you to see what you would not see in the ordinary. With this, you can help people find their given path and predestined route. This is The Gift that can dismantle deceitfulness and two-faced hearts."

His voice now became strong and firm;

"For the God I serve despises lies and falseness. No one will stand before Him without a pure heart. For it is so, that He, through His Spirit, is capable of transforming anyone whose heart wishes to be transformed."

"By the means of the Gift, I want you to reveal darkness where you see it. I want you to provide comfort for those who are filled with sorrow and give God's guidance of the future to those who are modest."

"*How* would that be done?" The question that had just hastily left my lips I could not justify once the shimmering creature looked at me with eyes of endless adoration. The very moment it became clear to Him that I had regretted asking it, He laughed. His long, golden hair fluttered like rays of sunlight around His face.

"Not by power of man can it be done, but by the power of His spirit" was His answer. The realisation that I hereon forward must learn how to seek His Spirit came over me with a sense of clarity I previously had yet to feel.

Lovely music filled the air around us. It sounded as if

billions of voices conjoined sang us a beauteous song. The music made me forget all doubts and uncertainties that had filled me before the Messenger had given me this task.

"I shall leave you now, but I will return to you to teach you more about the path you are destined to travel." He said before disappearing into thin air.

His words left me with even more questions than before.

THE PATH OF THE CALLING

On that day, declares the Lord of hosts, I will take you, O Zerubbabel my servant, the son of Shealtiel, declares the Lord, and make you like a signet ring, for I have chosen you, declares the Lord of hosts."
Haggai 2:23

Light-headed from all the information I had received I returned to my bed to rest. Shortly I fell asleep and began to dream. These dreams were always of the very different visions I would bring to the public.

While asleep, my stomach turned a knot of itself, partly due to the great dignity of the task, partly due to the fact that I, ever since His visit the other day, had not had anything to eat. It woke me up and made me want to look around in the kitchen.

The bright yellow hardwood floor creaked as my avid feet took me to the refrigerator. I could not for the life of me remember what I, before the visit, had stored in my refrigerator.

As I opened the refrigerator door, I noted that it was nearly completely empty. The exception was a large piece of bread in the centre of the fridge. Its' surface was golden brown and as I smelt it I immediately recognized the same undefinable scent as the one of the drinks from earlier that night; it was the scent of the mixture of honey and roses.

"Had He left food behind as well?" Filled with wonder and being too hungry, I was unable to resist having a bite.

Eagerly I broke off a piece of the bread and swallowed it indelicately. As soon as it was in contact with my tongue it melted, just how snow melts in heat. The flavour was unparalleled: warm and completely exquisite!

A sense of fullness filled me, and I experienced satisfaction spreading all throughout my being. I also noticed that the bread had not changed in quantity in spite of my intake. The bread appeared to have expanded to the same size that it had been at

16

the very same minute when I first had opened the refrigerator. The experience should have puzzled me more than it did. The many supernatural happenings I had experienced over the past day had left me nearly expecting more of the sort.

To my right, in one of the cooling compartments, I found a bottle made out of glass that I knew I had never seen before. The content was transparent and red: reminiscent of a bright, clear wine. The bottle had a V-shape, which allowed you to drink out of one end. Because I already filled by a great sense of discovery lust for the unknown, took my first mouthful from the bottle. The flavour reminded me of roses and snow, if by any chance you could describe a flavour as such. It was fresh with a delightful sweetness, although not too intrusive.

"Sweet Charity!" Whoever who had put the bread and drink there cared for me! When I had drunk myself void of thirst, I felt my exhaustion disappear immediately, along with the previous feeling of heaviness.

I then returned to my bed to reflect over everything I had seen and heard. Once I had lain down on my duvet, filled by a new sense of warmth and security.

"Maybe heaven had, in spite of everything, fallen down by me, Angela?" I thought, "Perhaps it was all just a hallucination in my consciousness; created by transmitter substances gone mad? In reality, maybe I am in fact just mental?"

However, an awareness so lovely and pleasant inside me could not be a sign of confusion. I chose to believe the Messenger's words about the Gift, that I had been given to administer. That idea led me into the deep rest where question marks were replaced by unseen wisdom; a secret nutrition that my soul now bathed in.

HOW IT ALL BEGAN

Your eyes saw my unformed substance; in Your book were written, every one of them, the days that were formed for me, when as yet there was none of them.
Psalm 139:16

he period before the messenger's visit had been a dark and lonesome time for me. Returning from work every day as a nurse at the psychiatric clinic in the town in which I was living made me feel heavy inside. All my life I constantly had been reminded of my past and somehow these memories had created a life for themselves inside my body. During the days when I was busy doing my duties, I did not feel heavy. I provided people with comfort, I offered them my advice and I signed them up with doctors. I felt how time passed me by at the speed of a ticking heart. The feeling of disappointment over how everything had turned out always came over me heavily in the evenings.

The story of my past was mostly about the time when I was married to André, André, who never really saw me, Angela. Who, as soon as he received his residence permit ceased to show me affection. I had always perceived myself to be a proud woman with good self-esteem, but with him I had slowly but surely started to feel invisible.

Angst squeezed me tightly whenever I heard him come home from work. I knew that it would turn into yet another evening of coldness and silence. However hard I tried I never received the love I was longing for. So today, whenever I looked at myself in the rear-view mirror I understand that his love was just as false as the smile he pulled on for his surroundings. In reality, his ego was so big that there was no room for anybody else.

I was reminded of my childhood, void of emotion, where on-par performance was the only thing that mattered in the eyes of my family. Only the memories from our family visits to Scania in southern Sweden could warm my soul. My grandmother lived there, and so did all her warmth and thoughtfulness. Memories from my great grandfather's bike rides with me also warmed my heart. He was such a kind-hearted person.

We used to bike to a store situated in a shed, near grandma's and grandpa's house. There we would buy Scanian gingerbread, on which we would spread thick layers of butter and eat with good appetite as we spoke about everything and nothing.

My great grandfather was a preacher in the Salvation Army and he often took me with him to meetings. My most vivid memories were of the meetings they held outdoors. My great grandfather would preach about God's goodness and grace. A great sense of security always filled me at those times. Whenever troubles in my family piled up, I always tried to create recollections of my grandfather; of how he, with his thick white hair, like a sky around his forehead, came bicycling to pick me up at my grandmother's. These memories were to me glimpses of happiness in the midst of that which oftentimes felt difficult.

I never felt as lonely as I did during the time when André and I were married. I was torn by the need of keeping my marriage afloat – to avoid failures– and the longing for a different life, where I could freely breathe.

I remember how tense I was after every workday; how the muscles in my neck and throat felt like iron. Sometimes André would have moments of benevolence where he accepted my request to give my tired muscles a rub. I enjoyed those times, but they were always followed by terms and conditions. He always wanted a dose of intimacy in return, and every time in a position where he was unable to see my eyes.

In my loneliness, I began to pray to the God, I had always imagined throughout my childhood. Every day I began by calling out to Him for help. At times, I would hold my rosary in my hand and pray for the Mercy of Christ and our Saviour.

Every now and then, a presence– a substance of love, completely unfamiliar to me– would fill my bedroom where I usually prayed. An undetermined anticipation of change would fill me. Words came into me; words that I never had heard before. A mild voice inside me would teach me that there is another road to walk.

I could not possibly have known then what would eventually

happen. I could not have known that everything actually could change. I could not have known that somebody had seen me and wanted to speak with me. How could it have gone straight past me that my steps had been predetermined and my life had been planned?

One night the truly strange thing happened, which I to this day cannot explain. It happened during a night like any other, where I as usual went to my bedroom after dinner and started to prepare myself for the night. As usual, I prayed for myself and for those who I held dear. In the middle of my words of prayer, I heard a soft voice:

"My daughter, I have heard your prayers and seen your tears. I have now come to you for your prayers' sake."

As I perceived this voice, love filled me. It was warmer than the sun and tenderer than any mother's arms. I fell to my knees in front of the bed table with the white rosary pearls. The room became light.

THE MEETING WITH BIRTHE AND THE BEGINNING OF SOMETHING NEW

Call to me and I will answer you, and will tell you great and hidden things that you have not known.
Jeremiah 33:3

*I*t had been a calm weekend before I took on the trip to Scania. I was invited to a female friend who worked as a deacon in an assembly in a medium sized town. Christine had yet to hear about my meeting with the Messenger and I myself was going back and forth between enthusiasms about what has happened and doubts if it had happened at all. Somewhere deep down I understood that I had experienced something very special and that I had been given by the shimmering, light creature had been a Gift that I was expected to administer to people out of goodwill.

The final kilometres I drove in my dark blue Volvo S40 felt surprisingly light and a still anticipation had started to settle itself in my entire being. Christine and I had talked about everything we would do during my visit; we would eat good food, have long conversations and even pray together. Both of us were looking forward to seeing old friends we had in common. Yet even so, I had a feeling that something else would happen. Perhaps this could be a trip where I would find use for what have been given to me by the hands of a rainbow shimmering Messenger.

I was awakening from my thought by my phone's ring tone. Should I pick up the phone or leave it? While I personally was against texting-while-driving, I had a strong sensation that this particular call was of importance and that made me forego my principle.

"Hello, Angela? Are you here soon?" The voice was that of my good friend Christine. "If you have a couple of kilometres remaining, change the route and meet me at Birthe's instead!" Birthe lived about ten kilometres south of the town where

Christine lived, in a full-size yellow house, framed by a fantastic rose garden. Upon hearing my question as to why we would meet there instead she explained:

"Birthe has entered in some kind of depression and wants us to come by to see her. Perhaps we can make her feel better?"

Birthe was a tall, vigorous yet elegant woman in her 50's. She had a complexion of a 30-year-old: light and porcelain-like with a youthful glow. The only thing hinting at her age was a couple of wrinkles around her mouth. Usually, Birthe was a dynamic woman with a love for discovering and travelling, as well as helping others. She was always gleeful and filled with a rare sense of curiosity; a trait often scarce amongst middle aged persons. Why this Birthe had been smitten with melancholy was beyond me. In some way, it felt as if this was a challenge to encourage her with the aid of the Gift.

When I drove into the yard by the large, yellow house dressed in rosebushes, Christine had already arrived. A big, warm embrace awaited me when I stepped out of the car and after only a few minutes of small talk it felt as if we had only been away from each other a short while.

Christine lowered her voice, almost as if to whisper something in my ear:

"Do you know? It feels as if something exciting is about to happen now; something we have never experienced before."

"I hope so." I answered shortly, before the door of the yellow house opened by Birthe.

"Welcome in." Her voice was low and mellow; not at all like Birthe's usual voice.

After having spent a while around the heavily packed coffee table– beautifully decorated and filled with sweet cookies and biscuits smelling of bitter almond– we sat down in the living room's cream-coloured English leather couch, giving us a chance to digest the sweets that we had just enjoyed with well-tasting, dark roasted coffee.

"I can't take it for much longer," said Birthe. "I need to get an answer; I feel completely empty and I no longer find the answers inside me to the things I want to know and look for."

She sounded exhausted and not at all like herself.

"Let's pray together and discover the answers to what you are looking for!"

"But – I do not want to say at all what it is about", she

continued. "I want it to be a divine answer to my questions; one of the ideas of God, not just a good idea."

Somewhat exhausted from the long trip I sank further and further down into the cream-coloured leather couch.
"The English sure know how to make good furniture," I thought to myself while I wondered how we would go about helping Birthe in her distress.

"Yes," said Birthe, "If I don't receive any reply from God that confirms that I am doing the right thing I will have to shut down the entire project."

The very moment she had said this, I thought to myself that it would be an impossible idea for us to try to guide her and offer her advice considering that she would not let us in on what was the matter with her. Nonetheless, because I, after my meeting with the Messenger, already understood that nothing was impossible for God, agreed to proceed with our prayers to find answers.

After nearly an hour of prayer and stillness, we started to feel tired. I could see in Christine's face that she had not either found anything to tell Birthe. I was headstrong enough to want to continue for a little longer and began to pray once more. Then a mild, divine and nicely scented wind came into the room. Birthe started to cry, completely still.

Inside my head an image popped up, at first somewhat blurry. Then I heard the voice of the Messenger:
"I want you to provide comfort for those who are filled with sorrow and give God's guidance of the future to those who are modest."

The image cleared up and it showed Birthe sitting with a white book with golden binders in front of her. In her hand, she held an ancient looking pen, with which she wrote in the book.
A sense of solemnity appeared until it became clear to me from looking at the words she had scribbled down that the book was a crime novel. Perhaps a little surprising in my mind considering that it was not very spiritual.

"I can see an image, Birthe. I can see you writing a book, and I can tell that it is a crime novel." My voice was shaking lightly as I told her, but I knew that the Gift was there for guidance for those who asked for it.
"Be brave and continue with your work, which is what you should do. It is pleasing Him."

When I had finished my final sentence, I could hear a joyful cry coming from Birthe.

"How could you have known? Ah, yes, I do know that it is not coming from you, but even so?" The joy was glistening stilly in her light blue eyes and she leaned forward to hug me excitedly.

"That was exactly what I wanted to hear and had I not been told that I would have shut it all down. Now I shall continue doing what I had started and now I know that it is right." She was as happy as a child was.

I too felt like a child at Christmas Eve. The Gift gave me joy as well, as it had not only given a human soul new courage but also because I had finally tested my wings in this new adventure: my "angel wings".

After returning from my trip to Birthe, I quickly returned to my day-to-day routines. The work at the hospital drained a fair bit of my time and energy, as did my relationship with André. I started to long more and more for moments, I could spend on my own with God and with the Messenger. I longed to spend more time on the spiritual journey I was going on. It felt like an important quest.

One evening after I had returned home from my work I sat down to pay the bills. I saw that the expenses were substantial in relation to my income and so I begged André to pay his part. This request was the start of a hot debate between the two of us. He did not want to contribute as he had too many expenses himself, he had said.

We began to argue. One word triggered the next, thoughtless words were entwined with agitation.

"My God, what should I do?" The thoughts travelled through my brain. "No, if you don't want to take on more responsibility for us it is better that we separate!" My words echoed in through our living room.

"Then I'll go," André said and suddenly he was dressed and on his feet. Before I knew what had happened he was out the door. He never came home again.

Later an acquaintance from his work came to pick up a suitcase filled with clothes that André had packed for himself while I was at work. Did I feel lament or sorrow? No, in actuality I only felt relief, possibly with a dash of dull melancholy.

It was silent and somewhat lonely in the beginning. However, after a while the silence and loneliness were just the things that to me became a precious treasure. Now I finally had the time for me that I had been longing for.

As soon as I was done with my everyday duties, I sat down to read from the Holy Bible and pray to Our Creator. My spirit went even more filled by a lovely sense of fullness. Even my appearance changed; my eyes were glowing with a still glistening– blue and grey– almost like light water streams. My soul could finally feel satisfaction.

One day when I was in a silent prayer as always, I placed all my needs before Him. My only desire was to satisfy Him and all of His wishes.
"Lord, what do You want from my life," I whispered over and over again. "What do You want for my life?"

That very moment, I felt the mild yet very lovely scent of roses from before coming to me like a mild breeze. I understood that He, the Messenger, was here.

"What do you have to tell me?" I asked, but before I had even finished the sentence, the words streamed into my spirit.

"My daughter, I want to bless you for your obedience. I want you to lay forward your wishes this very moment."

Obedience – That word felt somewhat alien to me, but I understood quickly that He must have referred to the trip I took to Birthe and the guidance I had given her on her path.

"I want to give to you what your heart desires," he said filled with adoration. Within me, one dream stood out especially, one that I had walked around nurturing for years.

I had seen an advertisement in the church I often visited. It was about a trip to India that would happen in the spring. The images in the travelling brochure fascinated me. It pictured large, light grey elephants and humans who rode them as if it was the easiest thing in the world, flowers in extraordinary colours and darker skinned people with large smiles on their faces.

I knew what I wanted to do. I wanted to travel to India! The trip there would be a combined pleasure and missionary trip. It would fit me perfectly, however... the cost of the trip was over 11,000 SEK, money that I did not have.

I understood that my wishes were important to Him and began therefore to pray that I, somehow, would be able to join the trip to India.

THE TRIP TO INDIA

Delight yourself in the Lord, and He will give you the desires of your heart. Psalm 37:4

The big jet plane took off from Arlanda Airport, left ground and began to climb into the sky. The increasing air pressure caused me conductive hearing loss. Underneath the plane, you could see the remaining splotches of snow on the Stockholm ground. "Soon," I thought, "We will be surrounded by quivering heat and exotic scents." I thought about how it had become possible for me to go...

One afternoon the phone had rung. It was Maja. Her voice had sounded excited:

"Angela, I am going to India in March!"

My heart had started pounding hard in my chest. As she described her trip, she described my dream.

"I am travelling with the church to take part in arranging a pastor conference in Northern India." My heart had pounded even harder.

"Maja, how wonderful! That is precisely my dream! How excited you must be!" After the conversation with Maja, my dream had felt strangely obtainable.

Then two weeks passed. Maja called me again Monday evening, but this time around, she started the conversation in an unusual way.

"Sit down, Angela! I have something to tell you." Upon hearing that, the first thought that popped into my head was that she was expecting. She probably also knew my opinion on the matter, which was that the four children she already had with her husband were enough for one lifetime. I followed her instructions and sat down in the chair standing in the hallway.

"Angela!" now her voice climbed into falsetto. "You are coming with me!"
"But – Maja, I don't have the money."

Maja's voice climbed yet another key:
"Angela, God is paying!"

The moment she uttered the words I understood that once again, surely my prayers were answered. Maja would pay for my part of the trip, she told me. In return, I would help her with her seven months year old baby Ivan that she wanted to bring with her.

Happiness knows no bounds. We arranged a Visa and apply of absence from work was easily granted. Expectations and joy murmured within me. The trip was a warm and emotionally filled adventure. The days, packed with planned outdoor expeditions. I visited Taj Mahal– one of the world's seven wonders–, rode on the back of an elephant and climbed a mountain hill. I travelled by train through India and flew from one place to another. Everything topped with lovely encounters with people, as well as purely supernatural experiences.

One day when we found ourselves in a middle-sized town in Northern India, I wanted to take a cab ride by myself, feeling a strong desire to visit a Christian church. When I reached the heavily trafficked street outside the hotel, I hailed a taxi and asked the chauffeur to drive me to the nearest Christian church.

"Oh, then it must be the Methodist Church", he said to me during the drive.

"Thank you. Drive me there, please." I replied.

As I reached the church, an odd sense of joy and peace filled me. Outside there was a beautiful garden. Inside the church I met a man, whom I at first assumed worked there as a janitor. We began conversing and he told me that his name was David. It was his church, but due to the persecution of Christians by the Hindus, he did not have many visitors. He invited me to come with him to visit his good friend, who was an owner of a publishing house and leader of the Christian members in the town. Following him felt completely natural and I felt safe in the company of David. He told me he was a government official and that his wife worked as a nursing assistant. Their two daughters studied at university, he told me.

The visit at the publishing house ended with a nice moment where we prayed together. I was also given a couple of books in English, amongst others a book by Stanley Jones, an English missionary. The meeting resulted in the establishment of collaboration between the Methodist Church and the church that I travelled with, making it possible for the Indian publishing house to get good literature from Sweden translated into English.

What wonderful pathways God leads us to! Still, even now when I think back to my answered prayer I can truly say that we do not have to rely on external circumstances, if Heaven wants something from us!

David and his family became my friends and we exchanged letters for many following years since my trip, establishing a valuable and beautiful friendship.

The dream of Taj Mahal, the expeditions to the exotic places with all their colours and smells, and all the warm and wonderful people I had met during my visit, all remained with me like a fond memory. Maja became a conduit for God's many purposes and she was willing to obey the call from Heaven!

THE JEWELLERY IN THE FOREST

I will give you the treasures of darkness
Isaiah 45:3 b

We humans are strange creatures. In spite of having climbed to the top of the highest mountain and gazed over lands spread vast, we may find ourselves from time to time falling into the pit, all because of our human limitations and the wounds to our souls.

One day I woke up sad and filled with woe, thinking about my strained financial situation, due to me being the sole provider of my family. In spite of all the wonderful things I experienced at the side of God and His Messenger, there were still days where memories from my dysfunctional relationship with André came over me.

Today was one of those days. I was longing to afford something beautiful to wear and to decorate myself. I have always had a particular fancy for jewellery. As far back as I could remember I had loved beautiful bracelets, necklaces and earrings to with I am gracing myself. I glanced over at my jewellery collection in my living room. There was not much there. Normally this would not be something that would boggle my mind; in my eyes, spiritual values were fare more invaluable than everything.

I decided to take a walk in the forest right by my block. I wanted to clear my mind and seek guidance from Him. In the dark, green obscurity of the forest, my dark thoughts all began to fade. I could feel the heavenly scent follow me on the path on which I was walking. I turned around to see if anybody was there—perhaps the Messenger. Within there was a desire to see His gorgeous, bright eyes and the love within them. Alas, there was no Messenger there, nor anybody else. In spite, I could feel a whirling stream of bright hope inside me. I felt a tingle –light like electricity– inside me.

As I was nearing the edge of the woodland, the sunlight glimmered over the pinewood treetops, resembling a Gloria. That is where I saw something glistening on the ground in front of me. I bent down to see where the luminosity came from. Right there on the ground there was the most beautiful green shimmering oval, encased in elegant golden ornaments.

I blinked and opened my eyes once more. Then I heard the familiar voice:

"It is yours now, for you are valuable." The voice filled with the handsomest tenderness said: "It´s for you, my daughter."

Filled with gratitude a wave of joy shot through my soul. "Thank you! Thank you, but I do not deserve this!"

"For you are so valuable." The words uttered again, although this time with a more determined fondness.

When I arrived at home after my promenade, I felt wealthy. It never crossed my mind that the jewellery did not belong to me or that somebody else had lost it. I only knew who had placed it in front of my feet on such a sorrowful day.

YOU GIVE THEM DRINK FROM THE RIVER OF YOUR DELIGHTS

They feast on the abundance of Your house and You give them drink from the river of Your delights.
Psalm 36:8

I s it possible to know anything about the future? Through the prophetic gift, can our previously opaque and nebulous inner vision be rendered clear and true? It had started to become clear to me that this only could be done through the transcendental grace of God. Some of my questions already had been answered.

This morning, my thoughts wandered on their own peculiar

paths. As I shared the Gift with Birthe, I had known deep down in my heart what she had needed, all thanks to the task given to me.

My dear friend Sophia had called me the day before and asked to come for a visit. She owns a summerhouse in my area and every year when she returns home we meet and enjoy each other's company. Usually, we converse and pray.

This was a year like any other. I was somewhat elated at the prospect of seeing my dear Sophia. She was a real angel, possessing a thick mane of long golden hair, a benevolent heart and an unparalleled humility.

While in prayer, I set the table. I knew the coffee was not that important to us, but it would still be nice to start with.

In through the door she came dancing, and with a big, warm hug, Sophia and I commenced our communion. After having coffee, we sang. I grabbed my guitar and started to play. Sophia's song – her voice clear and high – pierced the skies and opened the Heavens to our sight. We started to pray and we spoke about God.

"Listen, I've been pretty sick these last few days", Sophia said after a few moments of silence, "I've been having cramps, tinnitus, sometimes my ear would stop working and I could not hear anything on my left side. I've been feeling completely exhausted."

I believed her, even though her body confessed no such suffering. Her deep blue eyes glistened with tears.

"I know that He can hear your prayers. Pray for me, pray for my healing."
I knew that if I just revealed myself to the Lord, He would grant my sister His soothing balms. While I was praying, with power and strength, overwhelmed by a feeling of great certitude that Sophia should be healed.

The room filled with wondrous, intangible, sublime presence and sound. I understood that He was there to touch her. As I placed my hand on Sophia's head, she whispered excitedly:

"My head is becoming warm". Suddenly, I felt like a cloak laid upon my shoulders, and alien authority of prayer had been given to me, an authority I did not possess myself. After the moment had passed, Sophia turned her brilliant eyes towards me.
"Something's happened! He gave me something when you

prayed!"

I already knew that something had happened. We finished off with another prayer of gratitude and when Sophia left me some hours later, both of us uplifted by a heavenly presence.

Sophia contacted me a week later. She told me that the heat from my hand that she felt during the prayer had persisted for a couple of hours after her departure, healed and reinvigorated. Later on she had a medical exam and her doctor revealed her hearing was restored and that her tinnitus had completely vanished. The doctor was astounded and asked what had happened. Sophia had spoken of her faith in God and revealed that she had met someone with a precious Gift that had prayed for her.

We laughed and took delight in the miracle!
It was no mortal man that healed Sophia: It was He, the arbiter of his divine Gifts. He, who is dependent on mortal man to become the vessels, through which can be channelled His gifts throughout the world.

I was visited the same night. As I was falling asleep, I felt a presence smelling of finest rosebuds and there was a warm hand placed on my head.

"Do not forget to praise Him who gave you the Gift!"

This I solemnly swore and, in His gaze, I felt both small and infinitely important.
Some verses from the book of Psalms came to me before I drifted off into slumber: "And you make us drink from the river of your delights…"

After my meeting with Sophia, I understood the psalmist's words even better.

GIVE AND YOU SHALL RECEIVE!

Cast thy bread upon the waters: for thou shalt find it after many days.
Ecclesiastes 11:1

Everything that I have seen in God's creation; in nature, in every flower, in each seashell; in every exquisite creation, has given me such worshipful awe for my Father. He, who has made everything so beautiful.

I have come to love hand workmanship. For a while, I received inspiration to paint with bright aquarelle and gouache paint on flat stones that I had collected from the sea not so far away from where I lived. During this time, I painted the most beautiful angelical faces, brilliantly colourful, on wondrous white rocks as if within a dream. I felt as if I was supposed to provide a message with each stone; messages about God's love. On some

I wrote messages such as *"You are loved"*, on others I wrote *"Wonderful"* as well as other comforting words.

After having painted on about forty stones, I had the impulse of trying to reach out with the messages and the stones in a small neighbouring church. Said and done, the pastor granted me his blessing to arrange a small exhibition using the stones. About 50 % of the profit would go to children in South America. Everybody was happy with this arrangement, not to mention my satisfaction, I who literally has to see the words of Jesus come true: "I tell you, if these were silent, the very stones would cry out."

Not to long thereafter I was to travel to the capital in order to get my teeth done. I had packed lunch with delicious sandwiches and beverages for me and my two children, who were accompanying me.

When finally seated in the train compartment I noticed that I forgot to bring the packed lunch. A maleficent feeling filled me, for I knew how expensive it was to buy food on the train and there were many hungry mouths to feed. Silently I prayed that God, our Provider, would step in. I asked my children to follow my lead.

One hour later the train conductor entered our train

compartment and told us with a loud and joyous voice:

"The personnel who are in charge of the cafeteria wagon have not boarded the train, so today I will give each and every one of you whatever you want from the cafeteria!"

One inside I was filled with joy. Our prayers had been answered and from stones, there was bread!

So lovely is our Almighty, our Provider! For the remainder of the trip we were filled with a warm and joyful presence, one of that of the Heavens. Even today when I think back to this wondrous event, tears build up under my eyelids and warmth takes over my heart, because perhaps, in one way or another, the Messenger had played a part in this story…

THE EMBROIDERED WORD

Your word is a lamp to my feet and a light to my path.
Psalm 119:105

ne evening, in the company of good friends I visited a healing meeting. The preacher who proclaimed the words of God had put his hands on me and said a curative prayer. The reason for my visit to the healing meeting lay in the intensive longing for emancipation I felt at the time, especially for liberation from the memories of André that from time to time would cause me so much pain. My soul was so hurt, and no matter how much I spoke to God about it, it seemed as if the wounds would always tear right up. In my mind, I could not completely understand why this burden was something I would have to continue to carry even after our relationship had ended. However, God knew what I needed.

The heat of the day lingered in the air and outside the walls of the tent the August breeze quivered. This night murmur roared from the many people in the hall; the atmospheric excitement was palpable in the air.

The renowned Norwegian preacher began by providing a very vivid description of the Saviour's love and desire to heal us, his children, and how we should be retrieved. The preacher talked about the reunion and its' impact on us today. Within me, questions and yearning thronged together, leaving me with the sentiment of wanting to be free from the pain of my past, no matter what would happen next. My heart trembled and a stream of tears found its' way down my cheeks.
"Is this about me?" I thought.

Moments later, it was time for intercession and I hurried forth, my heart pounding through my chest. Not only was I in haste; I was forcing myself through the crowd, as did the woman in the gospels who had pressed herself forth to get a hold of the cape of Jesus so she might be cured. Finally, I stood before the evangelist, who now put his hand on my head and – without knowing me in person – said words about my life and my need for healing. Then finally! A stream of warmth and electricity travelled through me and I fell softly to the ground, my fall dampened by angels.

Once the meeting was over, I began to wonder and distrust. What had happened tonight? Was I free from the painful hold of my memories? Had my soul finally healed? The questions accumulated within me. "God, answer me!"

When I in to the parking lot by my house, I took notice of a small figure standing waving, using something that appeared to be a large piece of cloth. As I ran out of my car, I noticed that the figure was my dear friend Gertrude. In her hand, there was a big embroidery with a divine message for me. On the weave, sewed with beautiful, somewhat archaic words, I could read:

"From now on let no one cause me trouble
for I bear on my body the marks of Jesus."

What an answer to my doubts! Once again, overwhelmed by His great love I understood how He to a sceptic, can use His word, even in embroidery...
From that evening onwards the burden on my soul felt lighter and the heavenly balm began to heal my intrinsic wounds.

THE PSALM THAT TRANSFORMED LEONORE'S HEART

He leads me beside still waters. He restores my soul.
Psalm 23

The breeze was crispy this chilly springtime. I had just begun an assignment at the psychiatric ward in the southern part of the country, where I reluctantly stayed in a small room in a guesthouse. On my way home from work I passed a sign on the side of the road that said with shining letters: "Apartment lodging".

I shivered slightly and shuttered; perhaps because of the clenching cold, perhaps because of something concerning the glowing sign. In my bag, I found a pen and scribbled down the telephone number. Later the very same evening I called to ask if there was a vacant apartment for me to rent.

"Certainly, there is an unoccupied apartment", Leonore told me, "a small 2-bedroom apartment on ground level with a terrace."

In the midst of wary expectations, a peculiar joy bubbled inside me.

A week or so later I could install my belongings in the 2-bedroom apartment, which was facing a pond in a blossoming garden. I immediately felt a sense of homeliness and knew that this would ease the remainder of my visit.

One evening Leonore asked me to come up to her studio apartment, in the very top of her building. She had planned a concert with a very renowned director and wanted to share the experience with me in front of an enormous TV-screen. The genre of music was classical.

We had a very lovely evening together and we were offered good food and beverage by Leonore.

Leonore then told me that she for some time had found herself hitting a low point in her life and that she, during this dark time of illness, had called out to a greater power. This had happened while she was hospitalised after a stroke. She had suddenly experienced an old psalmody was opened. She described it as such, that *a hand from above had opened it* and that a particular psalm from the book had become *transparent and life-like.* This experience had given her new energy.

I gathered courage to ask if I could pray for her. Lenore told me that she would love to be prayed for. When I placed my hand softly on her shoulder, the words out of Psalm Chapter 23 became so vivid. I uttered them:

"He makes me lie down in green pastures. He leads me beside still waters. He restores my soul." The words came flowing over her, as a soft, invisible springtime rain and tears began to stream down her cheek.

"How could you have known?" she gasped.

"*He* knows everything and He loves you", I whispered in her ear.

When the time finally came for me to leave for the hotel, I was invited to a farewell supper in the studio apartment once more. This time I gave to her a glass framed picture, which I had had printed, displaying a pasture and rills of water.

On the day we bade our farewells Leonore showed me a glass table on which the painting was standing.

57

"This is now my altar where I pray the words of Psalm 23", she said.

A steam of gratitude filled me that evening; gratitude for the way by which He leads everything with His loving hand.

THE PURPURA COLOURED ANGEL

For He will command his angels concerning you to guard you in all your ways. Psalm 91:11

he time I had spent as a nurse at the ward was coming to its' end. As I was finishing up, folding my clothes into my small, black travel bag during the very last evening, I felt a pull towards my jewellery cabinet, where I was storing my ongoing jewellery projects that I had taken on constructing in my free time. What caught my eye was a purpura-coloured angel in glass and semi-gemstone: a glistering little creation in purple and white. My thoughts returned from time to time to this little angel.

"Why cannot I stop thinking about the angel?" I whispered to God throughout the evening, repeatedly.

Before I went to bed that night, I had a feeling that I was supposed to bring the angel jewellery the following day and give it to Anneli, who I had spoken to on many occasions during my visit at the ward. These were conversations, filled with spirituality and thoughts on God's visions for us. Anneli had experienced a vivid calling when she was young and had then travelled around as an evangelical within the borders of Sweden. She had told me about her calling; of how it had felt like a burning flame in her chest, but how it in later years might have started fading. When Anneli described to me how she had served in the kingdom of God, her blue eyes glistened with a rare brilliance. Her voice was clear and light.

The next day I gave the purpura-coloured angel to Anneli with the story of how I had felt in the deepest parts of my heart that it was a gift to her from the Father. Her eyes became shiny and it was clear that she was touched. With a low voice, she said; "You could not have known that I was given a purple-coloured angel, made out of amethyst, from my grandmother when I was young. I carried it around with me in my pocket for a long time and it made me feel secure and happy."

Yes, I had not been aware of this story. However, I knew that there was *Someone* Who had known it, and that this *Someone* had urged me to give it to Anneli, as a personalized message from the Lord of Heaven. How eager is not He, to watch us open our eyes and comprehend that He is a good Father and that He has such love for us human children... down to the smallest things!

LIFE, A GIFT

*Peace be unto you: as the Father hath
sent me, even so I send you.
John 20:21*

I t was the beginning of September and yet the heat of the summer remained. Golden leaves rustled in the garden. Inside of my heart there was a sense of anticipation: a mild stream. What this was I could not quite put my finger on. I knew however, that something lovely was about to happen. Even now, in my heart the visions were all still sleeping, like children in their mother's arms.

I had found myself under a walnut tree, where I used to sit and think. The warm wind blew enticingly through the garden and had a sweet and wondrous scent.

"What is happening?" My heart began to vibrate and my mind

filled with joy. The Messenger stepped over the garden's threshold.

"My daughter, oh how I have yearned for you!" His voice was joyous, yet somehow also melancholic, an utterly peculiar mixture. He began to speak:

"I have come to speak of the future and of why you have received the Gift."
A sorrow came over me as understood that perhaps this meant that He was to leave me. Tears were filling up in my eyes.

"You took part of a divine vision and the Gift was given to you for a reason". When He began to speak again, His voice became patient, like the voice of a father speaking to his little child.

"In the beginning was the Word, and the Word was with God, and the Word was God.' This was the Father's initial thought."

"Now I have come to you as a Messenger, for you to continue to carry the living Word, the bread which replete and never runs out, the bread from Heaven."

"You have been given part of the Gift and the divine calling so that you shall share it with those of the world you meet, the world which suffers more and more."

"Each morning when you open your eyes, open them in the ways of Heaven, from the inside and then up. Weigh your words as if on a scale. Consider what they create. Be considerate to those you meet, for they are made in God's image."

"Every person that you meet could be God in disguise, every situation you meet has a purpose and a resort. Every problem is a solution in the clever ways of Heaven and not in the way you would assume, but rather the way that God has planned. Therefore, always seek the Father's will, live off the voice and flow from the Holy Spirit in all situations."

"Give to the hungry food to eat. It is an important Gift; I have given to you, the Gift to see what I see, to speak what I speak. Continue to share this as a foretaste of what is to happen."
Now His bright, beautiful eyes filled with tears, salty as ocean drops.

"My daughter, receive the bread of Heaven."

In one of His hands there was the golden, fragrant bread I had tasted at our first meeting, I grabbed it, trembling. My hands were burning as if on fire.

"What is happening?" I exclaimed with a broken voice.

"Feed my lambs!" The voice was strong and piercing. "What you give is coming from Him, Who has sent me."

Trembling I fell to my knees.

"Receive the drink of Heaven!" Moreover, to me was given a golden cup, containing the shimmering liquid I had tasted when I first had met the Messenger; the drink, tasting of honey and roses.

"When you drink from this you become part of Him, He Who has sent me. Receive and drink!" The voice was warm, yet firm. The beverage ran down my throat and rendered me warm and strong.

"Your life is a Gift and what you shall do is part of the Divine Calling I have for you."

Then, when He breathed on me, I flew backwards in a soft embrace, resting in the heart of the Father and falling into a healing slumber.

The Messenger was still there and when I woke up and rose, He offered me a smile.

"My child, you are now strong and ready for the journey. I will leave you now and you will no longer see me, but you shall feel my breath now and then. You will know that is I who am there with you."

I stood up on my feet and – in an attempt to keep Him with me – I grabbed His shimmering cloak, however, in the very same moment, my friend the Messenger disappeared.

A scent of roses remained in the air.

EPILOGUE

What I have given to you is a tale, yet also something of the reality that is my life. I wanted to pass on part of the ethereal; a part of my Father's heart as He shows Himself in the Book of the Books, the Bible, where Jesus Christ throughout His life explained to us who the Father was.

You have a Gift, a calling, ability and a talent to minister. You are the carrier of a Divine spark: a Gift that only You can enrich the world with. Ask by prayer to learn more about which Gift You have been given. Often times it is what provides You joy that is Your Gift.

Your life is planned from the very beginning by God, even before He had laid the foundation for the earth there was a pattern of Your life. Heavenly visions were formed by holy hands, just for You.

Use your gift for happiness -for both humans and animals. You are unique and You are glowing. Enrichen the world with Yourself!

Listen to God's signals. God speaks in many ways, first, through the bible, but also via images or songs, as well as other signs that come from Him. Listen to the still voice inside of You.

Run with the vision from heaven! Do not let anybody or anything stop You. There will always be obstacles on Your path as You carry heavenly visions. They are there to be conquered!

God dreams when You dream. In your innermost rest Your secret dreams and visions. Capture them!

You are unique, and You are designed to shine in this world...

❖